POETIC REVERENCE

BY DOYLE RAYMOND

WestBow Press books may be ordered through booksellers or by contacting:

WestBow Press
A Division of Thomas Nelson & Zondervan
1663 Liberty Drive
Bloomington, IN 47403
www.westbowpress.com
844-714-3454

ISBN: 979-8-3850-0080-7 (sc)
ISBN: 979-8-3850-0081-4 (e)

Library of Congress Control Number: 2023910952

Print information available on the last page.

WestBow Press rev. date: 06/13/2023

WESTBOW
PRESS®
A DIVISION OF THOMAS NELSON
& ZONDERVAN

FOREWORD

WOW! The author is a poet indeed, but this literary work is so much more than poetry. From his mind to the pen and onto the pages of this book, wisdom, faith, love, and hope convene. The result is, some things we need to know that will truly "rejuvenate our hearts", and POETIC REVERENCE does just that – and you will not be shortchanged. Get ready for a lift and be empowered, encouraged, enlightened and yes, elevated!

Can these few pages do all that? Oh yes, they can and surely will. In almost every line, sentence, and paragraph, you will encounter Bobby Raymond's unquenchable passion to positively impact his readers with a deliberate determination to achieve a transformative outcome.

With much of this book written in the first person, you will encounter some personal experiences and testimonies of victory, hope, deliverance, and blessings. This is a different kind of high. A lift that is rhetorically designed to get you closer to God, guide you in the direction of your success, and point you towards your best life! Totally topical, POETIC REVERENCE covers a wide array of areas from time, talent and treasure, healthy eating, mothers, fathers, children, forgiveness, grace, and mercy, to the strength of womanhood and the power of fatherhood. It refreshes your spirit with Dr. King's dream and illuminates the continued effects of global warming on our remaining coral reefs. Intriguing indeed.

Welcome to this trailer-load of inspiration penned in these 40 or so chapters of bibliocentric, Christ-centered, lifestyle-focused, and heart-searching lyrics. And with each topic, there is a convergence of a theme, words of reflection, a prayer, and related scriptures.

This author is a man of words in the "Master's Hands", and the end result, is this book in your hands.

Read and rise to greater heights as you are reminded that "It is from the valley experiences that you grow, … soaring high above the mountains."

REV. DENNIS DILLON
Senior Pastor, Rise Church Global
Publisher, The New York Christian Times

Contents

PREFACE

Poetic Reverence is a powerful compilation of God Infused, Christ centered poems and reflections, that will empower your mind, encourage, and enlighten your spirit, and rejuvenate your heart. It is my desire that each poem, reflection, or prayer within this book, deeply touch the hearts and lives of each reader, in such a way that they may be encouraged to overcome current and future situations and circumstances. If it helps at least one person become closer to the Lord or strengthen their appreciation for this precious life we have, and ultimately, give their life to Christ, then my book would have accomplished its intended goal.

I have been quite passionate about poetry from a very young age, and just loved how the words seem to flow in symmetry to each other, with fluidity and grace. I would often go for long walks in the park close to my home and be in constant awe of God's Immense Creativity and Grace. How the beauty of the vast landscapes coordinates and cooperates with the many animals that calls the park home. The harmonious melodies of the vast array of birds seem to bounce off each other, as if a symphony orchestra is in constant motion. Such a sweet soothing sound to my ear, and a much-needed reset for my mind. Many of the thoughts and inspirations for the poems in this book, came to fruition, because of those priceless walks in the park. It even inspired the very title of one of the poems.

God has truly blessed me with an awesome family, who are also a key source of inspiration for my book. My wife and two kids are super energetic, immensely creative, and artistically inclined, each in their own unique way. I would often tell my kids to use the unique talents and abilities that God instilled in them, to bless others. My mother is also a tremendous source of inspiration and encouragement that has influenced this journey; therefore, it is with great honor and privilege that I use my God given talent and passion for writing, to be a blessing to others. It is truly humbling to know that someone would be encouraged or uplifted by one of my poems, and it is with great pleasure that I have this opportunity to share "Poetic Reverence" with the entire world.

IN THE VALLEYS OF LIFE

Lord, as you continue to lead and develop me, this one thing I have come to know …
Though I may walk high in the hills of life, it is in the valley experiences that I truly grow.

When my trials and tribulations seem so many, and my horizon looks as dark as the wings on a crow,
Please allow thy Holy Spirit to always remind me; It is in the valleys of life, that I grow.

Lord, I genuinely enjoy soaring high above the mountains …. Where the sun never ceases to glow…
But for me to reap this good harvest, I must be careful of the seeds I choose to sow.

I willingly surrender my past mistakes and weaknesses to You, so that the Jesus in me will begin to show, and the Holy Spirit Who Guides and Protects me, will continue to radiate, and glow.

Therefore Lord, I thank You for Instructing me, and leading me, in the way that I should go…. For it is not the highs in this life that defines me, but it is how I choose to operate, while walking in the valleys below.

REFLECTION: IN THE VALLEY

It is within our nature, as human beings, to enjoy those situations and circumstances that make us feel happy, fulfilled, content, encouraged or accepted. It is easier to operate in that environment where everything for the most part seems to be going okay. I remember reading about the long and tedious process it takes for a charcoal to eventually become a diamond, in that, it involves the charcoal being able to endure tremendous and continuous pressure and stress over a long period of time. Michael Larson once said, "A diamond is a piece of coal that stuck to the job".

In our relentless pursuit of success, we are driven by our respective passions and desires to achieve set goals and aspirations, but often lack the patience and endurance required to get there. We live in a society that craves instant gratification and intimately embraces the "I want it now" attitude, but also one that is so easily deterred by the pressure, stress, pain, and hard work required, for our dreams and ambitions to come to fruition. Anything in this life that is worth having takes time, energy, sacrifice, and relentless commitment. It is through trial-and-error situations that we learn from our mistakes and push towards building and perfecting our skills and ability.

The valley experiences in this life are designed to mold and shape us, to strengthen our character and build endurance. I often hear folks say, "I can't wait to get to the mountain top", without acknowledging the sometimes rough, rugged, and painstaking journey it takes to get there. Growth requires maintenance to effectively and eventually come to fruition. It is most certainly not an event, but a long-term process, that in most cases requires us to accept failure in some things, so we can truly embrace success in others. I thank God for my valley experiences, in that, those are the times that teach me to seek him even more, and to humble myself into asking and accepting the help of others who may have had similar failures or successes in their lives. Therefore, it is in the valley experiences of life that we grow.

Reference scripture: 2 Peter 3:18 (NLT)

<u>Prayer</u>

Precious Lord, I thank you for guiding and directing my steps through life. It is so easy to feel like giving up when trials and hardships come upon me, so please help me to remember that in those situations you mold and shape my character. Strengthen me in my weakness, so that you may get all the glory, the honor, and the praise. Amen.

I AM

Thinking about some of the things that they used to teach us way back in school, concerning black History......

They deliberately deviated so far from the truth to this day, those same teachings remain a total black mystery...

But hey, it's no surprise that the early teachings from generation to generation, got systematically

blurred and twisted, like some of the missing pages, where hundreds of thousands of slaves for sale, were listed.

We sometimes tend to forget that the oppression of our ancestors began way before the so called 400

years, when the soils of the earth and the sands of time, got soaked and penetrated by their constant fears and tears.

But fear is the opposite of faith, so we put our faith in the one who truly cares,

Yeah, that's our Father in Heaven, to stand up against Him you better not dare.

Those were the songs our forefathers used to sing, I am talking way before Booker T. Washington, Marcus Mosiah Garvey or even Martin Luther King.........

You see, their faith went deeper than the pain and trials they endured,

though oft times physically bound, yet in their spirit, like mighty eagles they soared....

The divine Agape love that God has for us, should never ever be ignored....

The Word of God declares in (Romans 8:35-37, NIV), "who shall separate us from the love of Christ"?

"Shall tribulation or trials, or persecution or famine, or nakedness, or peril, or sword?

As it is written, for thy sake we are killed all day long, we are accounted as sheep for the slaughter, nay,

In all these things, we are more than conquerors through him that loved us" …. (Romans 8:35-37, NIV).

Therefore, my brothers and sisters, our destiny and our worth can never be determined by any man,

because it was established, even before creation, by "The Great I Am that I Am ". So, let us claim what is

rightfully ours; more than a conqueror, I am, a mighty overcomer; I am, a redeemed child of God; I

am, destined for greatness; I am, a Kingdom Builder; I am, because He Is; I am, I am, I certainly am.

REFLECTION: I AM

History has taught us many things, some we may be able to relate to, and others we can only hope to learn from. As a nation, we have endured many trials and tribulations along this journey called life, yet our faith in God's Ability to Deliver us, still holds strong. Many trials were transformed into triumphs, stumbling blocks became stepping-stones and the setbacks were only a setup for our comeback. As far back as I can remember, my grandmother would always read her Bible, hum, or sing her favorite gospel songs or pray, especially when something bothered her. The resilient attitude and spirit she possessed was always a source of encouragement for me, and I still remember some of the stories she would tell me about the slaves having that same type of spirit. Amid countless struggles they encountered on the plantations, they would encourage each other through songs of praise or huddled together in prayer.

The Word of God declares in (Psalm 27:1, NIV), "The Lord is my Light and My Salvation; whom shall I fear; The Lord Is the Strength of My Life; of whom shall I be afraid"? (Psalm 27:1, NIV). This portion of scripture has been a fuel to the confidence of many a people across the globe; if we allow God to be our source of strength, then we won't have to rely on our own limited strength to get us through the tough times. The Great "I AM", is always there to Guide and Protect us and the magnitude of His Unfailing Love for us is hard to comprehend, but I will always be grateful for His Mercy and Grace. Never allow anyone to create your world for you, because they will always create it too small, and never let someone else determine your worth, because they will always place limits on it. Your worth was already established by your Creator; "The I Am that I Am"; Limitless in All His Ways; He Is, Therefore, I Am.

Reference Scripture: Genesis 1:26 – 27; (NLT), Exodus 3:13 – 14 (NLT)

Prayer

Thank You Lord for creating me in Your Image and Likeness. It is truly an honor and privilege to be called Your child and being able to demonstrate the character and goodness of Jesus Christ, my Lord and Savior, in all that I do. Amen.

LOVE

God is the very essence of Pure and Perfect Love, that Unconditional, Divine, and yes, that Agape Love. Mankind, the earth, and everything in it, were created because of that love; it was not generated by us here on earth, but was established by God Himself, in Heaven, way above. Even before existence ever existed, there was God, thus Love.

It is so easy for us to take His Precious Love for granted, as if it was some type of expressive tool we were handed; without it, mankind in sin, would be forever stranded. The Bible says, "For God so loved the world that He gave" (John 3:16 NIV), His Grace and Mercy to forgive us, even though we fell short and misbehaved. So how can there be love without giving, it's like the very source that permitted us to go on living.

Love is not something we gift wrap and place in a box or hide it away in a dark closet behind keys and locks; it's certainly not an emotion we use to outsmart others, like that cunning little fox. On the contrary, it is something that we should genuinely share and distribute, with tender loving care. There is no need to worry, so be of good cheer, because true love will always conquer fear.

I thank God for my precious family, whom I love and cherish dearly; the deep-rooted love and care we have for each other, regardless of situation or circumstance, continues to be strengthened, daily, weekly, monthly, and yearly.

Love is that deep earnest desire to give of oneself, so that another can benefit; that's the Character of Christ, yes, we can inherit it. So, let's get through this journey of life, by minimizing the disagreements, the fights, and the fuss, by making a solid commitment to love one another in unity, because God is the One Who first loved us.

REFLECTION - LOVE

One of the most abused, mis-used, and in some cases, under-appreciated word, that is shared between or exchanged amongst people, across the globe, is "love". Growing up as a young boy I thought of love as being something a boy or girl would tell each other, or something that makes a person feel like a million butterflies tickling them on the inside, and in essence, makes them feel good to hear someone say, "I love you". I can't remember hearing my parents say I love you to each other very often, yet I knew that they shared a deep love, devotion, and care for each other.

As a teenager, I became acquainted with many folks who would use that word loosely, "I love you to this", and "I love you to that", yet their attitude, actions and demeanor would demonstrate something entirely different. I would always hear my grandmother say, "God is love" and "Love is God", they are one in the same. God is indeed the true essence of Love. This earth and everything in it were created by God, for the purpose of containing man, whom He then created, out of His perfect love for us and towards us. Because of God's Love for us, we have the capacity and the ability to love one another.

Too often in our societies, love and lust seem to become paired together, as if they are one in the same. That could not be furthest from the truth, because love is the giving of oneself, for the benefit of another, even at the expense of self. Lust on the other hand, involves benefiting self or selfish desires, even at the expense of others. For some folks, love seems to be only skin deep, in that, it becomes so easy to fall out of love, as the threat of challenges emerge, misunderstandings, miscommunication, mistrust or mistakes. I remember there were times in my youth, when I would love and un-love people in my life, just as fast as I could say the word. I sure learned fast, that's just not the way it words.

Love is a deep-rooted source of strength that can overcome many obstacles that may come our way in this life. Feelings and emotions may come and go, but true love conquers and perseveres regardless of one's situation or circumstance. The Word of God declares in the Book of John 3:16, that "God so loved the world" (John 3:16 NIV), meaning that, every human being in existence will be saved, if we confess Jesus Christ as Lord and Savior. That's Agape Love. We all have this awesome and precious gift of love to share with each other, no matter what. Let us exercise this God given privilege.

Reference Scripture: John 3:16 (NLT)

Prayer

Precious Jesus, I thank You for loving me so much, that You would give Your Life for me. Please help me to love myself and to love others in the same way that You love me. I know many times I have harbored anger and resentment in my heart towards others, and I am sorry. Continue to be patient with me Lord, as I surrender my heart and life to you. Thank you for loving me and forgiving me. Amen

MOTHER

Who is a mother; a female intricately and delicately created by God's Mighty Hands; gifted with the ability to co-create life within, wired with maternal instincts and complex internal designs, that only she can somehow understand. A mother will fiercely defend and protect her child, even at the cost of her own life, persevering through all the pain, the triumphs and strife.

The tender care and unconditional love that she bestows, can almost mirror the Agape Love for us that God shows; the warm winds of compassion, she gently blows. I would often wonder, why did God choose Mary to be the mother of Jesus; the answer to that, no one truly knows. The songs she would sing for me, and the prayers she would send up to cover me, while I was still in her womb; helped to prepare me for entry into this world, like a bride excited to receive her precious groom.

I appreciate you, my mother, for all the deliberate sacrifices you have made, the building blocks for my journey through this life, you've laid; the many tears of joy that I witnessed, cascading down your face. There is absolutely no reason to hurry or haste, because your patience and kindness will guide me every step of the way; my gratitude and love for you, I will never, ever, delay. Mom, continue to walk in your divine purpose, and soar towards your destiny; you are God's Awesome creation, yes, incredibly.

So, to all mother's, I honor and salute you, both locally and far across the globe; may the Good Lord continue to strengthen and keep you and wrap you in the warmth of His Robe. I pray His grace and Tender Loving Mercies, forever be upon you; may His Peace that surpasses all understanding, always reside within you. I love you my dear, precious Mother, with all my Heart; I pray that the God Established Love and Bond we share, will never, ever part.

REFLECTION: MOTHER

Mothers in general holds a very warm and special place in my heart. I grew up being very close to my grandmother, who helped to raise me for the first few years of my life. From early on, I also developed a strong bond and closeness with my mother as well. There is a saying, "it takes a village to raise a child", so I am very grateful for all the mother figures that helped with my growth and development over the years. It is said that any female that is of age, can become pregnant with child, and possesses the ability to give birth to that child, however, it takes a woman of fortitude, character, and commitment, to become a dedicated mother. Under the right circumstances, giving birth to a child, should render any female the capacity and ability to embrace motherhood, should being the operative word. Of course, that's not always the case.

The true essence of a mother's unconditional love for her child, reminds me in some ways, of the pure, Agape Love that God has for us human beings. Regardless of the many mistakes and misfortunes that I have experienced throughout my life, my mother has always been a firm source of encouragement and strength, even when she had to discipline me for doing wrong, she always demonstrated her deep motherly love for me and towards me. The many sacrifices that my mother endured on my behalf, are countless, and I am extremely grateful for her patience and compassion when things got a bit challenging. I love and adore you with all my heart mom, and to all the mothers or mother's to be, across the globe, I salute you. God Bless.

Reference Scripture: Isaiah 66: 13 (NLT)

<u>Prayer</u>

Thank you, Lord, for my precious mother. Please continue to bless and cover her daily. She has always been there to love, comfort, and guide and encourage me. Always be her strength and her guide. Am

GOD'S MASTERPIECE

Who am I Lord, that you are so mindful of me; may I see myself but even a fraction of the way that you see me.

Your word declares that Your thoughts of me out number the grains of sand, for I would be a lost soul if you should release me from the grasp of your mighty hands....

Your blessings upon me are too many to count, and you fuss over me in ways I can't truly understand.

I am humbled that of all your creations, you declare me your most prized possession, and the seeking of your presence, my most cherished obsession.

By your hands, I was fearfully and wonderfully made; from the blazing rays of doubt, you are my eternal shade.

Thank you for loving me in ways I can't comprehend and for the saving of my soul, Your son Jesus Christ You sent; out of obedience, in serving You, I will obediently go the full length.

I appreciate Your goodness, kindness, and Your Grace; during times of darkness, let Your Light ever shine upon my face; through the many trials and difficult times in my life, You are always able to secure me within Your Wonderful space.

The peace that You have instilled in me, surpasses all understanding, and Your Relentless Faithfulness gives me the courage and strength to stand firm, withholding nothing.

Father, you are my Rock, my Guide, and my Fortress; Thank you for creating me, Your Masterpiece and Your Prized Possession.

I am truly humbled and Blessed, beyond what words could ever, possibly describe or make an impression.

REFLECTION – GOD'S MASTERPIECE

The way we see and know ourselves, is by far, much different than how God sees and knows us. Our limited capacity to truly comprehend the depth of His love and care for us, makes it extremely difficult to grasp the magnitude and vastness of His grace. The only way to truly get a sense of how God sees us and shows His love for us, is by reading his word. The book of Ephesians tells us that we are Gods masterpiece, and again in the book of James chap.1, which states "And we, out of all creation, became His most prized position" (James 1:18, NLT).

Every individual must be able to believe that word for themselves, for it to become a reality in their lives. It surely humbles me to the point where I must now re-access how I think about myself. Society today tends to categorize communities and the people living within them, by their physical attributes, possessions, social status, and the size of their bank accounts. Growing up, I observed many corporations and governmental entities, determining the value and worth of a person by their established "net worth". The misconception is that someone with a high net worth, and a popular social status, is of more value to a community than the person who is deemed to have a low net worth or social status.

It is my hope and prayer that each person reading these words will come to a better understanding of God's love, and compassion for them. We did absolutely nothing to deserve his love and grace, yet he holds us in such high esteem. It is my goal to encourage and motivate others to read God's word in order to know him on a more intimate level, and to truly understand how much He loves and Adores us; His Prized Possession and Masterpiece.

Reference scripture: Ephesians 2:10, James 1: 18 (NLT)

Prayer

Thank you, Father God, for creating me, loving me, and blessing me with your awesome grace. I am humbled that you choose me to be your masterpiece, your prized possession. May I never consider myself any less than what you say I am, and please help me to be the example of your goodness to others, so that they may come to understand who they are in you and know their true worth, because of you. Amen.

CHILDREN OF TOMORROW

Who are the children of tomorrow? They are our precious sons and daughters, God's awesome gift to us, so they can secure the future; then why are there so many children in our world today, experiencing much heartache and sorrow; some are abandoned, some bruised and abused, some manipulated into warfare and some that are forced to steal or otherwise, permanently borrow. Unlike the occasional scary movie that is over in about two hours, there are children living out their young lives, in the reality of sheer horror; yes, that is the transparent actuality of many children of tomorrow.

Let us therefore be the parents, relatives, guardians or caregivers, who will diligently help to eradicate these negative and destructive elements that affects our children in such potent ways; the seeds that we plant into their lives today, will eventually become fruits that will help nurture, develop, and protect them for the future ahead, even unto the end of days; our children are here to stay, so let us be that beacon of light for them, like the sun and its energizing rays.

As parents and guardians, we should make it our priority to build the platforms and create the environments that will promote healthy living, stimulate critical thinking, and provide fun activities that will motivate their energy and creativity; we will never, ever, force upon them, generational curses, customs, rituals, or institutionalized captivity. On the contrary, we will choose to love them, teach them, embrace them, and most definitely, sacrifice for them, because they are indeed a tremendous blessing; like having that healthy, delicious, and nutritious salad, topped with your absolute favorite dressing.

Our children of tomorrow are right here with us today, so let's create safe home environments and surroundings, where they will always have a place for their little heads to lay; being careful how we respond to them, or what we choose to say; their growth and success, we will never delay, because our precious children of tomorrow, are destined for greatness, in each and every way.

REFLECTION: CHILDREN OF TOMORROW

There's a saying that applies to parents worldwide; "having a child, is like having your heart walking around outside of your body"; it's like having a little piece of yourself, literally walking around each day. Whatever affects them, good or bad, directly affect you in return. I would often hear my son say "dad, I'm a mini version of you", a simple statement, yet very profound, especially when it comes from a ten-year-old, as he was at the time. It tickles me to hear him say it, and it keeps me in check each time I think about it; what am I reflecting for my children to follow. We must be so ever careful of the seeds we choose to sow, because they will surely impact the next generations to come. As parents, the process of raising a child is rich with emotions, uncertainty, joys, sorrows, trials, as well as triumphs. Whether you are a mother, father, grandparent or guardian, there is an endless well of comfort and fulfillment in watching a child grow and mature into a wonderfully complex, yet unique young adult and onwards.

I believe that my wife and I are somewhat protective over our children, without making the mistake of sheltering them from the realities of life, be it emotional or social. Kids should be allowed to be kids, in every way possible. They should be afforded the environment to play safely, make friends and learn from their mistakes. It is all part of the growing process, difficult and complex at times, yet very rewarding. It truly upsets me when I see or hear about incidents that involve children being mistreated and taken advantage of, or being physically, emotionally, or sexually abused. I can remember a few times while walking on the street, or riding in the train, where I witnessed a parent or guardian cursing profanity while rough handling their child. One can only imagine the horrors that may take place in such a household, behind closed doors, if that same type of attitude and behavior is being expressed in the open public.

The Word of God declares in Proverbs 22:6, "Direct your children onto the right path, and when they are older, they will not leave or depart from it" (Proverbs 22:6, NLT). I am surely a testament of that portion of scripture, because growing up, I was disciplined so many times, but my parents always let me know why I got the belt or the rod, each time I stepped out of line. Love would always be demonstrated in my household as a child growing up, as it is within my own household today. My children will always be corrected and instructed in such a way that love will remain the center of our lives, and in everything that we do together.

Reference Scripture: Proverbs 22:6 (NLT)

Prayer

Lord God, I commit and surrender my children to you, because they are Yours. Thank You for blessing my wife and I with our precious gifts of a son and a daughter, whom we cherish dearly. Please help us to continue to be a source of love, provision, inspiration, and protection for them, and for the village of family and friends You have provided to help us raise them. Amen.

ESSENCE OF A WOMAN

In the beginning God created man, then out of man He created woman; not just solely for the man but for all mankind, a co-creator of life, she is awesome. The woman is fearfully and wonderfully made, intricate, unique, meticulous, yet mysterious in all her ways. You are God's trophy, lifted high for the whole world to see, that's why women have always been an integral part of our world history.

She is wired with an inner strength that has conquered isolation, interrogation, rejection, abuse, sexism, racism, criticism, stigmatism, and any other type of "ism" you can think of. She is versatile and spontaneous, possessing all the ingredients that perfect dreams are made of.

The woman was created to withstand the pressures of time, like a charcoal pressed and stressed only to be revealed as a precious diamond, oh yes, a one of a kind; precious woman, you are so fine. Created in the very image of God, your reflection is pristine and divine. Woman, embrace your essence and demonstrate it with your presence.

Make it known that you are a joint heir to His Kingdom, for He has already reserved your permanent residence. Display your beauty, vigor, and endurance, let the world see the nature of your character regardless of the situation or circumstance. You are destined to prosper and be a success in whatever you do, because God's Love, Strength, and Peace, will forever empower you.

REFLECTION: ESSENCE OF A WOMAN

God has truly blessed me with an abundance of strong women in my life, from my childhood to this very day, and I am grateful. My mother, my wife, sisters, aunts, cousins, and family friends, all played an integral part of my growth and development. These women and so many others were the inspiration behind this poem: *Essence of a Woman*. I truly salute my precious wife, Yvette, for being the anchor and cornerstone of encouragement and inspiration in my life. No doubt, the struggles of women have been tremendous even from the beginning of time and continues even to the present time. Their resilience and determination to overcome, has been the backbone of many families including my own, and the drive that propels our society across the globe.

Women are so unique in their own mysterious in their own respective ways, but the mindset of a strong woman to overcome the very obstacles that try to overpower them, will remain the same even to the end of her days. They were created and hotwired in such a way that strength is derived out of challenges, triumph is acquired from the strongholds of trials, and success is chiseled from the stumbling blocks of past failures. So, woman, embrace your Creator and walk in the Fullness and in the Presence of His Character. May your journey continue in power, peace, prosperity, optimal health, and well-being. God bless you all.

Reference Scripture: Psalm 45:5 (NLT)

<u>Prayer</u>

Lord, I thank you for the strong women you have placed in my life who has helped to shape and mold me, encourage, and direct me. Please help me to continue to love and appreciate them, and I pray a special blessing to all women wherever they may be. Amen.

FORGIVENESS

Why is it so difficult for us humans to simply forgive; the pain and the hurt goes ever so deep, it often dictates the type of life we choose to live.

When circumstances entice us to take, take, take, yet we struggle with staggered reluctance, to just let it all go and freely give.

The bitterness will fester, if we only operate by way of feelings and emotions; as if someone forced us to drink a cup full of the un-forgiveness potion; can you feel the notion. The more we give of ourselves to others, is like inheriting a quality-of-life promotion.

Well, the first step towards healing, is learning how to release, by taking all your burdens and troubles to Jesus, and leaving them at his feet. Allowing Him to fill your heart with His compassion, mercy, and peace. When I hunger and thirst for the right way of doing things, He invites me to the table of forgiveness, so I can graciously feast.

So yes, it is at times hard to genuinely forgive, but remember, even before the beginning of time, though we were all unworthy, and because of His Immeasurable love for us, God still chose to give. Therefore, let it be reflected and demonstrated by the way we think, what we say, and how we simply choose to live. Forgive, forgive, and please again, forgive.

Reflection - Forgiveness

One of the hardest things to do in this life, is to genuinely forgive those who have caused us much hurt and pain, whether physically or emotionally. The deep hurt that has taken root in our hearts, may seem quite difficult to release, let alone, forgive. We must be able to first admit that there is a hurt or pain to begin with, to set the platform for release and forgiveness to eventually take place.

As a young boy, I found it very challenging to admit when I was feeling hurt or disappointed, and realized that the lack of release would eventually cause resentment and malice to build up to the point of contention. God shows us in His Word that He chose to forgive us even when we did not deserve His forgiveness. He gave His son Jesus, to die for our sins, so that whoever believes in Him, shall be saved.

With that in mind, let us make the tough effort to forgive that someone who may have wronged us in some way, in the hope that we ourselves may be forgiven for our own wrong doings. A verse in the Lord's Prayer declares "Forgive us, our trespasses, as we forgive those who have trespassed against us" (Matthew 6:12 NMB).

Reference Scripture: Matthew 6: 12 – 15 (NMB)

Prayer

Lord, please help me to forgive others, in the same wat that You have forgiven me. I know that it's not an easy thing for me to do, but with Your continued help, I will be able to forgive those who may have wronged me in any way. Amen.

DR. KING'S DREAM

Dr. King profoundly declared in his own words "I have a Dream". His desire to see the vast boundary of racial divide mended and sealed, from seam to glorious seam. To see the bountiful occurrences of social injustice come to a permanent cease, as the seeds of unity and peace flourish into a beautiful increase. He had a dream that one day the color of our skin will not determine our future or destiny when our social or economic stature will no longer prevent us from achieving or gaining the same opportunities. To behold the harmony of seeing children of all colors and creed playing in the same courtyards, having access to the same education and schools no matter how hard.

A dream to see the erected pillars of bias fall and crumble, in the same way the mighty thunder in the skies would roar and rumble; when the seeds of hate and discord begin to shake and stumble. The God of all creation loved us so much that He gave us all His one and only Son. His favor is not bestowed upon us according to the color of our skin because He created us as equals; all as one. That's the way He designed this world to operate, even before time begun.

Working together, we as a people can eradicate the stench and decay of racism and the discrimination that leads to racial divide. If we continue to expose the festering disease of social injustice, behind walls of shame and guilt, we no longer will hide. So let us love one another, embrace each other, build up and edify one to the other. Let us live in harmony and peace so that the love that God has placed in our hearts will multiply and increase.

REFLECTION: DR. KING'S DREAM

To this very day, Dr. King's speech "I have a Dream" still resonates deep in the hearts of many people across the entire globe regardless of race, creed, or social economic backgrounds. In the simplest of ways, Dr. King desired to see every man, woman, or child to be treated as equals. He desired to see the deliberate and premeditated racial injustice, mistreatment, incarceration and senseless murder of black men, women and children alike come to an end. Oft times I would imagine how my grandmother with whom I was very close lived as little girl growing up in those days. I remember her telling me stories about her childhood that made me cringe and, in some ways, made me feel anger towards those who made her feel any type of anger, pain or sadness.

Dr. King's Dream Speech tore down barriers and racial divides that dominated his era and beyond. Unfortunately, his "Dream" is still unfulfilled, in that racial injustice, unprovoked bias and the savage mistreatment of "people of color" still surges to this day. Yes, we have come a long way but there is still much work to be accomplished, to see the absolute fulfillment of that dream. It will continue to take a conscious and committed effort on every individual's part, every home, community, borough, state, country, and continent alike to treat each other with respect regardless of our differences. We almost promote equality in every area and sector of society and allow growth to take place without prejudice of any kind to fester or contaminate the growth process. Can this be accomplished? YES IT CAN: if we all allow the "God in us" to guide our thoughts, actions and character that will in turn fuel and promote the necessary changes "amongst us", then we will certainly begin to see the results multiply "between us". Our attitude will always determine our approach, so let us all hold each other accountable and watch the miracle manifest. God Bless us all.

Reference Scripture: Isaiah 1:17 (NLT); Micah 6:8 (NLT)

<u>Prayer</u>

Lord God, I have seen racial injustice and unfairness all around me and at times it does anger me. I pray you strengthen me where I am weak, help me to forgive those who have hurt me and be a pillar of strength to those who are oppressed and in need of encouragement. Thank you for your grace and mercy upon me. Amen

38

HOPE AND FAITH

The word of God declares that "faith is the substance of things hoped for, and the evidence of things not seen" (Hebrews 11:1, KJV), but what does that really mean. It means that the very things that I am believing God for, even though not presently with me, will soon by faith come to be, calling those things into the present, as if they have always been. The unattainable or the impossible has no meaning to my God, because in Christ Jesus, I will always be able to win.

In the most trying of times, when all things seem far and lost, I will not despair, because my Lord and Savior has already paid the price on the cross; though many things in this world may try to intimidate and overtake me, I know who orders my steps and who is the Boss. The raging storms of this covid-19 catastrophe has drained the faith and depleted the hopes of many, yes, new fears awaken; when families across the globe become dismantled, like a mighty earthquake, their lives were uprooted and shaken; the grief and sorrow unbearable, each time another life is taken.

Despite the immense challenges of it all, we must hold fast to our faith that better times are yet to come, as we move to the rhythm and beat of God's Celestial drum; believing in the hope of tomorrow, as we sing praises to our Heavenly Father, song after glorious song. Be of good cheer because we know to whom we belong, unbreakable and together strong. There will always be someone or something that will try to press the pause button on your hope, or slowly chisel away at your faith; but let your confidence reside in the Lord, who is your strength, because good things do come to those who wait. To be crippled by the fear of uncertainty, we will not take the bait, because our lives and future is secured in His capable hands, at a constant rate. It is never too late, so please take this God given opportunity to exercise your hope and activate your faith.

REFLECTION - HOPE AND FAITH

No doubt, these past two years 2020 and 2021, have been the most challenging and daunting, to say the least that the United States and other countries across the globe have ever seen or experienced, period. The raging storms of Covid-19 and its mutating abilities have caused much havoc and destruction, massive loss of lives, families displaced and dismantled, healthcare systems and facilities drained and depleted of vital resources, hope and faith hammered at every angle. The pandemic has tested the best of us who continue to hold on to the ray of hope that much better times are coming, and the steadfast faith which decrees that out of many tragedies, there will be triumph.

I have come to realize that it is much easier to have the posture of hope and faith, while being eagerly optimistic, when things seem to be going somewhat okay, but the moment tragedy strikes, the real test of one's capacity to apply hope and faith begins. When you find yourself way out on a tree limb, with high winds tossing you back and forth, having absolutely nothing else to hold on to, but your faith, hope, and trust in God, that some type of rescue will come, will truly challenge your resilience, steadfastness, and your belief that better times will come. Yes, it is easier said than done. One of my greatest and dearest motivators, is my mom and her story.

In early 2020, not long after the pandemic and citywide shutdown began, my mom and dad who lives by themselves, somehow contracted the covid-19 virus. My mom who is a full diabetic and heart patient, got it the worst. This feisty, super energetic woman became weak and frail in her body, unable to move about as she once could only a few weeks' prior, due to her constant lack of appetite and other mild symptoms. My dad on the other hand, who is always a fighter, helped her back to health, and by the Grace of God, they both conquered the virus. However, Months after recovery, my mom began to develop blood clots in her body, particularly in her lower abdomen and legs. She eventually lost her left leg to diabetes in 2021, yet her faith in the Lord remained strong, as she used her walker to get around the house. The chronic pain and discomfort that began in her remaining right leg became tremendously hard for her tolerate, and soon had the leg amputated due to clots and lack of blood flow. Even with this life altering setback and daunting challenge, not just for her, but our entire family, my mom told me that she believes that she will walk again, by the Grace of God, and with the aid of prosthetics. Her attitude since then has been one of hope, prayer, and optimism. If that isn't an absolute declaration and demonstration of hope and faith, then I don't know what is. I love you mom with all my heart.

Reference Scripture: Romans 15:13, Hebrews 11:1 (NLT)

Prayer

Thank You Lord for giving me hope, and for being the very reason that my faith remains strong. I know there are times when I worry and complain about my circumstances, but You always make a way out when there seems not to be one. Please help me to stay encouraged and to be a source of encouragement to others, Amen.

SILENT, SILKY BUTTERFLY

Sometimes I would spread my soft blanket over the plush comfy grass and daydream about being a little closer to the clouds. Their varied patterns of white and grays dancing across my eyes so fast. I would flutter over building and trees, sometimes in near collision with some of the birds and the bees. My movements unstable, yet stealthy as the strong winds blow me in directions I never intended to flee. Yes, I am beautiful, soft, and delicate, unique among the other millions just like me, yes, I am that silent silky butterfly, can't you see?

The colors of my wings are a sight to behold, patterns of yellow, burnt orange, blue, black and dots of white and I am just too soft to hold. They are quite mesmerizing depending on the angles illuminated by the rays of sunlight, and if you are not too careful, my reflection could obscure your line of sight. I must keep on moving, got no time to waste, my life cycle is very short, so excuse me if most times you catch me in a haste. Sometimes flying hundreds of miles to find a mate and quickly procreate, so that the next cycle of larvae can begin to generate.

Oh, this life of mine is short but sweet, so I must now rest on this flower, get a taste of delicious nectar, recuperate, and eat. My life's journey is quite complex, exhilarating, yet extraordinary to say the least. I remember crawling on my belly clinging to the limbs of trees, while eating my way thru as many plants, fruits, and leaves; storing up as many calories and energy to facilitate the next phase of my journey as if I collapse and wheeled away on nature's gurney. Plunged into utter darkness and cocooned into sheered stillness, my body disintegrating then miraculously reshaping and regenerating into a new form of spectacular visual greatness.

Wow! I no longer must crawl on my belly or wiggle into the leafy abyss. How marvelous is this God given process called metamorphosis. I can now spread my wings even though no one really taught me how to fly. Yes! Here I am world, behold, the silent, silky butterfly.

REFLECTION: SILENT, SILKY BUTTERFLY

The metamorphosis from caterpillar to butterfly, is one of the most iconic, intriguing mysterious and complex transformation in nature. As far back as I can remember, butterflies have always captured my interest and picked at my curiosity to the point of becoming a somewhat nurtured obsession. I remember as a child, I would pretend that I was a skilled and famous butterfly hunter; but that title was so far from the truth because as I would find out time and time again, that butterflies are extremely hard to catch especially with two tiny hands. Now, as an adult, the illusive butterfly still fascinates and intrigue me. From the mesmerizing kaleidoscope of radiant colors and patterns on their wings the sheer number of different species is astounding. The very fact that this beautiful creature was once crawling and wobbling around on its belly eating every leaf, plant, grass, or flower in sight. Yes, the sometimes creepy, caterpillar.

The life cycle of a butterfly is quite interesting and fascinating to say the least. All butterflies start as tiny eggs, each about the size of a pin that the females deposit on leaves in small clusters. The eggs typically gestate for up to two weeks at which point they hatch into butterfly larva or what is commonly known as the caterpillar. In fact, almost all insect species go through larval stages, the fly for example in this stage are known as maggots. The caterpillar must now consume massive amounts of food in the form of grass, leaves, and other plants materials that allows them to grow up to one thousand times their original birth weight. There is a purpose for this eating madness. The caterpillar in all actuality, is preparing for the next stage in its life cycle when it will put all those calories to use, for the purpose of powering a startling and mind-boggling transformation.

The pupa stage is where this marvelous transformation takes place. Inside a chrysalis, which is the last expression of the caterpillar's exoskeleton, is where incredible processes are occurring. The body of the caterpillar completely breaks down on a cellular level, and then reorganizes itself into a new form. After a few weeks, an adult butterfly emerges from its encasement of darkness, and almost instantly has the capability and capacity to fly. In this final stage of its life cycle, the adult butterfly spends most of its time searching for a mate to sire the next generation. Ironically, after going through such a complex process of development, the butterfly doesn't have much time to display its diversely awesome and unique beauty. Upon reaching adulthood, many species of butterflies live for less than a month. It always baffles me as to the reason why the caterpillar would go through the magnificent transformational process of metamorphosis, becoming this spectacularly gorgeous creature, with the result of having such an extremely short life span; but as the adage states, "that's life".

Reference Scripture: Genesis 1:20 – 24 (NLT)

Prayer

Lord, I thank you for being the Father of Creation. Even the animals and the insects reflect Your Glory, and the Creative Genius that You are. The butterfly in fact speaks to Your Authority over life and everything in it, and its transforming capabilities. I appreciate You Lord, and all that you do. Amen.

THE FAITHFUL SHEPHERD

The Lord is my Shepherd, what more could I possibly want; He guides me and directs me and keeps me safe from harm.

In the cold chills of life, He always provides the right blanket to insulate and keep me warm; even in times of distress, when anxiety and fear seem to overwhelm or intimidate me, His mighty Word reminds me of His promises that soothes my spirit and gives me the courage to remain calm.

Though many times I've strayed, He always reassures me of His kindness, His mercy, and His grace; His Rod and Staff, they comfort me and keep me in my rightful place.

My Shepherd feeds and nourishes me, so I may become healthy and strong, though sometimes I trespass and graze in restricted pastures, He lovingly corrects my wrong.

I am so filled with thankfulness and joy, my gratitude soaring high, like the glorious melodies of an Angelic praise song.

Thank you, my Lord and Savior, for Your tender loving care, that propels me to walk by faith and never in fear. Your Precious and immeasurable Love insulates and protects me, Your Spirit in my heart, I will always hold dear.

You willingly gave your Life Lord, to save mine, therefore, I will praise you forever, even beyond the end of time.

Reflection – The Faithful Shepherd

In the hustle and bustle of today's urban societies, it is difficult to even imagine the tremendously important role a Shepherd performs in assuring the well-being of his flock of sheep. In most cultures, shepherds usually tend or herd sheep, but there are other cultures in which they take on the added responsibility of herding flocks of goats, but either way, their primary responsibilities remain synonymous. They must safely lead the sheep to their destined feeding pastures to graze and ensure a good source of drinking water. The Shepherd must constantly monitor his flock, to prevent some straying away from the group, and simultaneously keep a watch for sneaky predators.

The Bible relates to Jesus as "The Good Shepherd", the one who guides, feeds, protects, and watches over us, His Precious Flock. The Book of Psalms, chapter 23; "The Lord is my Shepherd" (Psalm 23:1, KJV), Puts into perspective, the vast responsibility of God being our Good Shepherd. I believe that each person who reads this passage of scripture, must identify with it, in their own personal way. It took me a long time to truly understand the example of God being my shepherd, but as I grew in my relationship with The Lord, it became crystal clear that He is indeed my Guide, my Protector, and the One who sees to all my needs. At times when I become stubborn and disobedient or stray from the path that He has laid out for me, I am guided back into place by His Mercy and Grace.

Reference Scripture: Psalm 23 (NLT)

<u>Prayer</u>

Lord, You are my Creator, my Shepherd, my Strength and my Redeemer. The One who guides and directs my life in so many ways, even when I don't deserve it. Thank You for being patient with me in the times when I want to do things my own way or when I choose to stray away from the path You have given me. I appreciate You Lord, and I humble myself to be obedient to Your leading. Please continue to guide my steps, so that I will be able to help others along the way. Amen.

THE COST OF FREE WILL

Does it really matter what I say or how I choose to say it, or will it make a difference what I think, and how I choose to apply it; does the choices that come my way each day have eternal consequences, when I exercise my right to use them, any which way I see fit? Well, you better believe it does, every bit, by little, bit. Sometimes the pressures and challenges of this life can impede upon our feelings and emotions that influences and drives our thought processes; the result at times, makes us feel like the composers of erratic, distorted melodies.

The Word of God declares that "life and death are in the power of the tongue" (Prov. 18:21 NIV), so please be careful of what you say, because your words can either produce life or bring death in the long run; yes, that negative energy you entertain, can literally destroy your dreams and aspirations before they've even begun.

God has blessed each human being with the gift of free will, though many may choose to misuse or abuse it, as if it's some giant, self-fulfilling hole, they're trying to fill; He'll never, ever go against your will, nor anything in you, forcefully instill. Therefore, let's be mindful of the words, thoughts, and decisions we make, way before our mouths begin to spill.

May we prayerfully and humbly submit our own free will, as His to fulfill, then watch as our words and choices, bring life to all that is ill; surrender in obedience to the Lord, and in His Presence, be still. Allow God to guide your thoughts, direct your steps, and influence your ways; everything you do with your life should bring Him all the Honor, Glory, and Praise. Even Jesus Christ, God's one and only Son, prayed and said," Not My Will Father, but Thy Will, Be Done" (Luke 22:42 KJV).

REFLECTION – THE COST OF FREE WILL

God has graciously given each and every one of us human beings, the gift of free will; the ability to make our own choices and decisions, as we see fit. We often tend to gravitate towards doing things our own way, whenever or wherever, and to think, there are some places in this world, where people are unable to exercise this God given gift of free will. They are denied the opportunity to speak freely, have their opinions and choices debunked, and are unable to vote for basic human rights; yes, there are some of us who often take this gift for granted.

Those circumstances do not diminish the fact that each of us were ordained this gift, however, there are many choices we can make, that can bring harm and ultimate destruction to those around us, and yet, there are choices that can encourage, edify, uplift, and stimulate life in others. There were many times throughout my life when headstrong stubbornness got the better of me, and I decided to do things my own way, even when some of those things ended up hurting others in my life. God desires a relationship with each of us, and expects us to surrender our lives, thoughts, actions, and even our will to Him. If we choose Christ, we ultimately choose life everlasting, because Jesus is the way, the truth, and the life; on the other hand, if we decide to go through this life without accepting Christ as Lord and Savior, we are essentially choosing eternal death. That's in fact, the hard truth.

Let's therefore make the right decisions that will empower our own lives, as well as those around us, our families, neighbors, friends, and communities alike. The choice is yours; I choose life, regardless of my situation and circumstances, trials, or triumphs, and I cannot do it based on my own strength or will power. It will happen only to the degree that I surrender and submit everything about myself to God. I pray the same for you all.

Reference Scripture: Psalms 143:10 (NLT)

<u>Prayer</u>

Father God, I am sorry for the countless times that I chose to be selfish, stubborn, rebellious, and unappreciative of all the things You have done for me. Please help me to depend on You more and more each day, and to be an encouragement to those around me, to try and do the same. Amen.

THE STORM AND THE RAINBOW

Sometimes the toughest and most challenging situations and circumstances that we encounter in this life, are somewhat like raging storms, and in other instances, a never-ending fight. Like a ship being tossed back and forth by massive waves, regardless of its well-built strength or might.

Pushing against the strong winds of anger and fear, like a rain-soaked blanket, holding you tight. Though you may feel lost in the void of the darkest night, just put your trust in Jesus, and He will lead you into His Glorious light.

In the same way He commanded the raging storms to be still, He will do the same for you, if you but surrender to His will. When I feel empty and depleted, with Your Comfort and Grace, my heart You'll fill. May Your love color my life's palette, like that of a rainbow, Your very Presence in my life, causes me to radiate and glow.

Yet, the very trials we face, are designed to mold, and shape us, and help us grow. "The Battle Is Mine", sayeth The Lord, so let's be careful of the seeds we choose to sow. Jesus Christ Is the Only Way, The Truth, and The Life, so in case you didn't know before, now you know, that's just the way it goes.

It is said that there is a light at the end of every tunnel, so in this one truth I know; Like the Covenant He Made with Noah, at the end of every storm, God will surely provide the assurance of a majestic rainbow.

REFLECTION - THE STORM AND THE RAINBOW

When we think of a storm, the pictures that may dominate our minds are that of torrential rains, high gusty winds, immense flooding, tress being uprooted and such. As a boy growing up in the West Indies, I know a thing or two about getting caught up in a major storm. Scary to say the least, but even scarier is the realization that some of the situations and circumstances we encounter in this life, at times feel like the elements of an actual storm. It is no doubt easy to crumble under the overwhelmingly intense pressures of the moment, even to the point where some folks may entertain suicidal thoughts.

The resilience and capacity for us as human beings to withstand such pressures are astounding, yet without the ability to foresee most of the turmoil that may eventually come our way, puts us in a vulnerable position. The Word of God assures us that Christ is our refuge and our Fortress, a very present held amid our most treacherous storms. Relying on our own self efforts will get us but so far, instead we are encouraged to seek God's Presence and Strength, even as we struggle to push our way through these many challenging, life altering, stormy circumstances.

In the same way that a rainbow appears at the end of each torrent storm, we are reassured that God will always make a way out for us. There will be triumph at the end of each trial season, though some trials we must endure for the purpose of building our character and resilience. The rainbow signifies hope for a brighter tomorrow and increases our confidence and ability to press beyond the pain and discomfort and accomplish all that God has established and intended for us. There is no life without difficulties, but we must be steadfast and committed to ride out our storms, seek help where we may need it, and turn to the Word of God for guidance, encouragement, and direction.

REFERENCE SCRIPTURE: Psalm 107: 28 – 31 (NLT)

Prayer

Lord, I thank you for always being there for me, especially through the difficult times. I know there are times when I feel completely overwhelmed and depleted by the stormy circumstances that come my way, and sometimes give in to the depressive thoughts that follow. Help me to always be quick to place such situations into your capable hands and continue to lead and guide me in the way that I should go. Also, please allow me to be a source of encouragement to others who may be weathering their own storms. Amen.

THE GREAT SUNRISE

In the wee hours of the morning, I peered through my bedroom window, examining the seemingly

endless, slate grey skies. With the heavy tingle of sleep still lingering in my eyes, I stared into the distant

horizon, in eager anticipation of that glorious sight; none other than the soon to emerge, great sunrise.

The luminous colors of burnt orange, yellow and deep amber, performing a fiery dance before my eyes,

bringing fountains of pleasure to my now awakening sight. It's as if this mighty ball of fire is being pulled

up from the earth's core, by majestic strings of light.

It effortlessly burns away the gloom and darkness of night, in a battle for radiance, it hardly needs to put up a fight, thus introducing the world to God's Awesome creativity and Marvelous Light.

It's unchartered and unmatched energy fuels and sustains life as we know it, humans, animals, plants and trees, all scramble to retrieve and bask in it.

Not much in this world can parallel the beauty and sheer brilliance of the great sunrise, each unique in its own spectacular way. In this truth there are no room for lies, the luminous rays of sunshine covering the land, like a giant swarm of flies.

So let your hearts be of good cheer as you embrace the words of the wise; with the going down of every sunset, comes the glorious dawning of the great sunrise.

REFLECTION – THE GREAT SUNRISE

A sunrise is such a distinctly picturesque thing to see. Imagine the sun slowly rising and dancing its luminous radiance across the horizon, as if being slowly lifted by the Master Himself. There is nothing that captivates my attention more than the awesome spectacle of a rising sun, I can hardly count the number of pictures of sunrises I have taken throughout the years. There are so many places I have visited, where the sheer beauty of nature completely blows my mind, and being an outdoors enthusiast, it's always a tremendous delight to be in the midst of it all.

It's very easy to be in total awe of God's Creative Genius, by simply looking up into the sky. That magnificent canvas, painted with mesmerizing cloud formations and designs, blended with the blue streaks of the sky beyond, with the backdrop of the mighty sun rays reflecting and piercing through the thicket of grey, off-white and sometimes pure white clouds. As a child growing up on the island of Jamaica, I would oft times wonder if there was some type of invisible rope or chain of some sorts, that God used to pull up the sun from beyond the mountains.

Capturing the very moment that the disc of the sun peeks above the eastern horizon, is a sight that is permanently imprinted in my mind, and is joyfully repeated in different ways, for every sunrise I am fortunate enough to see at its peak. The sun in and of itself is a fascinating phenomenon, in that the power and energy at its core is both unchartered and unmatched by any other source of energy in the universe. A Solar Flare which is an intense localized eruption of electromagnetic radiation in the sun's atmosphere, can travel for millions of miles, even having the ability to disrupt or knock out power grids and communication portals on earth. God is Awesome indeed. The great sunrise will always be one of my favorite sights to behold.

Reference Scripture: Habakkuk 3: 4 (NLT)

Prayer

Father God, You are indeed a Creative Genius, the Master of all creation. Thank You for the opportunities I have had to bask in the wonder and splendor of Your beautiful creations. I am in awe of every sunset and sunrise, the majestic sight of the full moon, the grace of each waterfall, and the gorgeous landscapes. Please help me to always appreciate Your goodness and kindness towards me, and to never take anything that You have created for granted. Amen.

TIME, TALENT, AND TREASURE

Lord, I have made up my mind, to commit to You, my time, talent, and treasure; the very thing in this life that brings me joy, fulfillment, and beautiful pleasure. Even the trials and tribulations that seek to discourage, devour, and destroy me, I also give to You as my act of sweet surrender; because You, Lord, have the power and authority to turn bad situations around, for the good, according to Your loving Grace and Splendor.

Every gift, talent or ability that You have instilled in me, You did so that I may be of service to others, though sometimes this very act of service seems like quite a bother; may I never be too busy or preoccupied, to not extend myself to those in need, be it a sister or a brother; furthermore, I am blessed, so that I may in turn become a blessing to another.

How can I feel comfortable keeping the precious time you have allotted me, all to myself, without committing a part of it to You, each and every day; I was fearfully and wonderfully made in Your Image, so it is my utmost desire to represent You Lord, in each and every way; I am sorry for the times You were denied the first fruits of my treasure, when all along, it was You my God, Who provided the resources that gave me access to the pay; and how can I keep quiet, the testimonies of all the times You have delivered me, without opening my mouth to say, thank you Lord, for showing me the way. Please let every aspect of my life, bring You all the Honor and all the Glory; it will be my greatest accomplishment, to share with the entire world, the good news of Your story.

Reflection: Time, Talent, And Treasure

Have you ever felt as if you have all the time in the world, to do whatever you want, when you want, with whom ever or wherever? Well, I sure have, countless times at that, but to my dismay, that could not be further from the truth of things. We are all on borrowed time that was graciously given to us, by God, our Creator. Believe it or not, that's the way it is. I cannot begin to count the occasions that were spent wasting time on idle or insignificant things that were unfortunately for the most part, selfish desires. There were other times that I certainly misused or underutilized my God given talent and abilities, to say the least, and most definitely, been stingy with my treasure, be it money received in the form of gifts, or was acquired as payment from different jobs throughout my teenage years.

As I began reading the Bible about how Jesus shared whatever little he had with others, or how He encouraged His disciples to do the same, not to mention, how He willingly and graciously, suffered and gave up His life for me, so that I could be forever free, inspired me to look deep into my own life and how I chose to live it. I first had to realize that the time I have really belongs to God; secondly, I had to identify what my God given talent and abilities are, so they can be used to inspire others. For example, I have always enjoyed writing and cooking from a young age, now, as a chef and poet, I can use these abilities to bring upliftment, pleasure, and service to others. Once we fully recognize that every good thing in us and about us, is a blessing from God, it becomes easier to be a tremendous blessing to others, by sharing our time, talent, and treasure. The best part of those, goes to God first, so that He will always get all the Glory, Honor, and Praise, from our lives and livelihood.

Reference Scripture: Luke 12:34, 1 Timothy 6:17 (NLT)

Prayer

Precious Father, You have blessed me with so much, even when I don't deserve it. Thank You for the Mercy and Grace given to me each day, and for the gifts, talents and abilities bestowed upon me. Please forgive me for the times that I have been selfish with my time, talent, and treasure, knowing very well that they come directly from You. Allow me to be a blessing to others as I strive to please You each day. Amen.

WHO IS A FATHER

A father should be the cornerstone of his family, the rock, and very pinnacle of stability; He is the discipline practitioner, the protector, and the dedicated provider; He keeps them safe, tight, and secure, like that of a container; a man created in the Image and Character of God, Who is our source and Sustainer.

A father would give his life to protect his family, amid eminent danger; the one who will nurture and develop his children, and never in their lives, become a total stranger; his attitude and focus are rock solid, like that of a dedicated ranger.

A father should never be an oppressor or a divider, nor should he ever become an abuser or an unfaithful suiter; may the Holy Spirit be his guide and constant reminder. The very presence of a father should stimulate an atmosphere of confidence and security; his words and actions should mirror his creative ingenuity, in the same way that his lifestyle and social networks, should encourage healthy and productive comradery.

A committed father will desire for his children to become better than he ever was; to stimulate and encourage them with the strength and steadfastness of a father's love`, coupled with the tenderness and compassion of a precious dove; He will always put the needs of his family above his own, his sacrifices and hard labor for them, will forever be written in stone.

I will always love and appreciate my father, who has been there for me since the day I was born; for me he was willing to tackle life, by the reigns and the horn, his wall of trophies and accomplishments, I will earnestly adorn. A crown you shall forever wear, for all that you have done; so please be assured my dear father, that you will always be loved by your one and only son.

REFLECTION - WHO IS A FATHER

Growing up, my father was always a "mister fix it all ", whatever the issue or the problem, whatever was broken or damaged, my dad could somehow fix it. He was a mechanical engineer by trade, and it seemed like everyone knew that repairing car engines and other machinery was second nature to him. Most of his friends that had car trouble would ask my dad to help them solve the issue. As a young boy, I distinctly remember my dad coming home from time to time carrying large rolls of paper under his arms, and when I asked what they were, he said they were blueprints of our new house. I would often hang with him in our back yard, by his makeshift work bench, where he would cut, chisel, and assemble the wood for the picture window frames that would eventually be installed in our new house. From blueprint to what is now a tremendously beautiful house, my dad helped to design and build it from scratch.

A creative genius he is, and I am very proud of all that he has accomplished, not just for himself, but also for his family. Throughout the years, we have had our ups and downs, but without a shadow of a doubt, my father has always been there for my mom, sister, and myself, regardless of the situation or circumstance, even to this very day. My father has always been that pillar of strength and stability in our family, the one we can always call on and count on, when things happen to get a little sticky. My heart is filled with such gratitude, even now, as he attends to my mom's every need, during a very difficult and challenging time for my family. My mom lost both her legs to diabetes, and my dad is her round the clock caregiver; it speaks volume about the ultimate commitment to one's marital vows "For better or for worse, in sickness and in health, till death do us part". After some fifty plus years of marriage, my parents are still there for one another, in love and unity. Pop, I honor and salute you, and love you with all my heart.

Reference Scripture: Psalm 103:13; Proverbs 3: 11 -12 (NLT)

<u>Prayer</u>

Precious lord, I thank you for blessing with an awesome father. Please continue to strengthen him and keep him, especially through this challenging season. He has always been a source of provision and protection throughout my life, and I am grateful. Help me to be that rock in my own children's lives, as he has been in mine. Thank you for loving and blessing him.

YOU ARE WHAT YOU EAT

There is a principle that states, "what you don't learn from the first time, you are destined to repeat"; so please don't take it lightly when I say, you really are what you eat; Healthy food choices does indeed lead to healthy living, it's like a precious gift, to our own bodies, we're giving.

To perform this task, it shouldn't feel like a burden or a tedious chore, but something we should be willing to do, more and more; If our health "Lipid Panel" numbers seem to be less than favorable, let's do the right thing and better the score; the more you're committed, the more you become sure.

Some types of food will help you gain great health and wellness, while others unfortunately, may lead to a moment of silence and stillness; yes, some food types out there can literally kill you, whether in the short term, or over a long period of time; yes, the right food and health lifestyle, may even encourage all friends and families, yours, and mine.

This is the hard truth that each of us, must find a way to digest; foods that are high in fat and cholesterol, can and will, overtime, lead to all kinds of sicknesses or disease; the ball is in our court, it's all in what we choose to do, that will eventually put our hearts at ease.

So, let's get educated about the types of foods that are best for our bodies, in time, and with much practice, it will become as easy as performing our favorite hobbies. Therefore, let's exercise wisdom, and do the right thing; eat right, drink right, sleep right, and most definitely, live right, because that's the song we will forever sing.

Reflection – You Are What You Eat

Growing up, I would hear this saying, "you are what you eat", but thought nothing much of it. Whatever I felt like eating, or more likely, whatever food, my grandmother or my parents had available on any particular day, that was it, no question about it. The truth of the matter is diabetes, heart disease, and high blood pressure is quite prevalent on my mother's side of the family. My great grandmother whom I never knew, my grandmother to whom I was very close to, and my mother, all had history of these deadly diseases. My grandmother lost both of her legs to diabetes when I was very young, and my mother recently lost her legs to diabetes as well. This generational curse must be broken, and it can and will be.

Some aspects of these types of diseases are hereditary, but for the most part, the majority can be prevented if certain dietary and lifestyle changes are implemented vigorously. I worked as a chef for many years, preparing all types of cuisines for restaurants, catering events and tastings. I would also eat whatever I felt like eating, whenever I wanted to eat it. In 2013, I suffered a full-blown heart attack that shook my world, and that of my family.

Thank God that I am here to testify about it this day. I am grateful for life, and the very things that matter the most. The foods that are high in saturated fats, cholesterol, and elevated levels of starch and carbohydrates, can be quite harmful to our bodies, especially if consumed over long periods of time. So yes, we are what we eat. The right kinds of foods can indeed promote healthy living and longer life spans, for many who may have otherwise fallen victim to these deadly diseases. With discipline, steadfastness, and the right attitude, we can achieve healthy lifestyles, wellness, and the peace of mind to enjoy life to the fullest.

Reference Scripture: 1 Corinthians 10:31 (NLT)

Prayer

Lord, please help me to make the right decisions about my health and wellbeing. To choose healthier foods and drinks to put into my body, ones that will not harm me, but allow my body to become more energized and healthier. Thanks for the many blessings that You have given me. Amen.

A WALK IN THE PARK

How awesome it is, to take a nice, invigorating walk, run, or stroll in the park, be it in the morning, afternoon, or even after dark; there are so many things to do and to see, I just don't know where to start; the tranquility and peace that my mind and body receive, is simply, just a matter of the heart.

The scenic journey continues, my hungry eyes eagerly soaking in the amazing plethora of trees, vast arrays of exotic plants and foliage, in all their different colors and splendor, yes, a magnificent work of art, nature at its best, to its beauty, I helplessly surrender; my absolute favorite place to jog, hit the bike trails, throw Frisbee with my kids, or just simply lay on a blanket in the shade, and absorb all that my lovely park has to render.

No matter the season, the park is always bursting with life and fun filled activities; be it family and friends gathering for a picnic, folks prepping for a tasty barbeque, or local artists chilling in a musical jam session of lyrical creativity; yes, it's time for a sip of peace and tranquility. Even the turtles seem to agree, as they sit in unison on the rocks, soaking up the sun, with their heads raised high, as if saluting the Creator in all His Majesty; indeed the park is an oasis of multicultural diversity, where folks from all walks of life can comfortably interact, mingle, cuddle, or simply hang together in sweet connectivity; a spectacular scene where love is the center piece, with no room for adversity.

It feels so good at times, to just sit by the lake and bask in its immense beauty; the perfect setting and platform to reminisce, reset and be in awe of God's Creative Genius, yes, His Perfect Ingenuity. The pure white swans and muti-colored ducks adds to the already picturesque scene, as they graciously glide along the surface of the water, the sun's rays reflecting their gorgeous colors, the true essence of humility. Thank You Lord for providing me with this awesomely incredible space, where I can come to escape the hustle, bustle, and noise of the busy streets; where chaos transforms into quiet and peace, a place to rest my mind, and get an overdue relaxation treatment for my weary body and feet. So yes, as you can see, the neighborhood park is one of my absolute favorite places to be.

REFLECTION – A WALK IN THE PARK

Nature is one of God's beautiful creations. Through nature, God can teach us, speak to us, connect with us, and provide for us; how awesome is that indeed. As a young boy growing up on the island of Jamaica, I would always prefer the great outdoors, rather than spending most of my day inside the house. I would usually play around in the backyard with my friends or eagerly go on tips to the bush trails or walk to the mountains that surrounded the community, with my cousins or my uncles. So naturally, the park is one of my absolute favorite places to go, and it is the same with my kids as well. If they had their way, we would be in the park every day of the week. During the seasons of spring, summer, and fall, my kids and I enjoy riding our bikes throughout the park, often trying to discover new bike or hiking trails; we also love to roller blade at the awesome skating rink located in the center of the park and enjoy throwing Frisbee or prepping for the occasional picnic or barbeque with friends.

It is so fulfilling to see the multitude of ethnic diversity throughout the park, people interacting and having fun by indulging in the vast array of activities available. I have enjoyed some of the most memorable musical and cultural events right here at my favorite Prospect Park, in Brooklyn, New York. People from all walks of life are always in abundance, no matter the season, there is always something to do. Even the winter months have their unique perks of ice skating, snow sculpting and snowboarding. The frozen lake is always a sight to behold, the geese and swans waddling their way across the frozen surface. The fall season is always a spectacle to behold, with the majestic foliage and their alluring colors of yellow, burnt orange, reds, and pale greens; some of my favorite pictures in the park are taken during this festival of falling leaves. So there you have it; a walk in the park for me is a different fun-filled and relaxing adventure each time, regardless of the season.

Reference Scripture: John 1:3, Psalm 96 :11-12 (NLT)

<u>Prayer</u>

Father God, I thank You for being the Creative Genius that You are. I appreciate the times I spend in the park talking to you, hearing from You, and basking in the awesome beauty of nature and everything in it. Thank You for providing my every need, and please help me to never take any of it for granted. Amen.

LIFE AS USUAL, ON THE REEF

As far back as I can remember, my life began as a rush and then a race, only it was at a somewhat slower pace. I remember seeing thousands of my brothers and sisters scrambling frantically across the vast light brown sand, as if they were the mass crowds jamming to their favorite rock band; a sight so immense, it was hard for me to immediately understand, if we did not make it quickly enough to the water, life, and death for us, went hand in hand. The seagulls and other hungry creatures were just waiting to gobble us down, one by one; being born into an environment this treacherous is really no fun.

Finally, into the water I go, a tiny Hawksbill turtle swimming for its life, oh boy, it will surely take quite some time for me to grow; I feel so lost in this endless void of water, what lies ahead in the distance, I really don't know. Keep moving forward, keep moving forward, I kept telling myself, not sure in what direction to go, but somehow my instincts are driving me to find a place that I can call paradise, if there ever was such a place in this massive body of water; oh, right about now, my tired self is in desperate need of a tow.

After swimming for what seems like weeks, or months even, who knows, I noticed several schools of fish, sporting vivid colors of red, yellow, blue, orange, white and black striped, rushing to somewhere, as if late for an appointment or something, guess that's the direction in which I'll go. Far in the distance, I could barely see what looks like that place of paradise I eagerly sought, a vast ecosystem that supports hundreds of thousands of marine lives; a place where there's food, shelter, safety to grow and become stronger, and finally, no more hunger or strife; who would have thought, my very own reef paradise, bursting with life.

This place is far more amazing than what my imagination and instincts led me to believe; it looks like an endless city metropolis, its frantic energy I'm ready to retrieve. The colorful yet strange looking plants that move together in harmonious symphony, the coral formations that gather in large batches, some small, some medium, and others gigantic, all-in effortless symmetry; their patterns and colors seems like an underwater art extravaganza, with fishes swimming in and out of them quiet skillfully, like the hustle and bustle of people on a busy street plaza. I think it's time to rest a bit, and put something in my belly, since discovering these creatures known as sea sponges, soft and delicate, yet not quite like jelly, but very yummy.

Each morning the sun pierces through the surface of the water, illuminating this majestic reef city; its inhabitants scrambling about as if perceiving the chores that lay ahead for the remainder of the day, oh what a pity. Some gathering for breakfast, some looking moody and mean, others simply goofing around and creating a scene; guess that's why they are called the clown fish team. There is never a dull moment on the reef, like a tropical rain forest under water, a place of beauty and dreams; but this majestic oasis of mine began to take a turn for the worst it seems. After many years, the temperature of the ocean began to increase, way beyond the comfort level of the residents, soon the tranquility began to cease. Even my own body started to respond in strange and different ways; burning sensations and dizzy spells would be the length of my days. This once vibrant and lush ecosystem began to decay, unusual colors followed by slime, swept across the coral bays; shades of purple, dark brown and eventually, the scary looking ghost white, amplified by the sun's rays. My precious corals, bleached beyond its ability to fight off this terrible climate change, has forced many of the inhabitants to go find another reef oasis to claim.

Reflection – Life as Usual on the Reef

I have always been intrigued by the sheer vastness and hidden mysteries of the world's oceans. Its unobstructed and unapologetic openness speaks volume to the astounding beauty, source of power and energy, and the unparalleled depth of the great and mighty ocean. As a matter of fact, the combined masses, in terms of volume and depth of the world's oceans, coupled with all other bodies of water, could perhaps come close to being compared to the utter vastness and endless void of space. Even more fascinating, is the majestic and mesmerizing array of marine life, teething beneath the surface of the deep; yes, particularly, in and around an oasis known as coral reefs. Coral reefs are thought to be the most diverse ecosystem on the planet, providing habitats, shelter, and a countless supply of food, for thousands of marine organisms. The Great Barrier Reef is the world's largest coral reef system, which is composed of over 2,900 individual reefs and 900 islands, stretching for over 2,300 kilometers that covers an area of approximately 344,400 square kilometers. Massive to say the least, this great reef is located off the east coast of Queensland, mainland, Australia.

Many fish spawn on the coral reefs, and juvenile fish spend much time there before venturing out into the deeper waters, where they will eventually mature. Hundreds of thousands of marine species live in and around the reef, like fish, sharks, eels, shrimp, lobster, crabs, and sea turtles, are just a few of the multitude of creatures that rely on the reefs for their survival. Food and living spaces are usually up for grabs or defended fiercely, depending on the situation at hand. One species of sea turtles, the Hawksbill, can affect reef diversity and succession, by simply eating. These turtles prefer eating sea sponges above anything else, which is helpful to maintain a high coral cover on the reef. Coral reefs are not only a vital part of marine life dependence, but reefs also protect coastlines from wave actions and storms and are an important source of revenue for many nations, through tourism and research expeditions.

Coral reefs are like the tropical rain forest of the ocean, because just like plants and trees that provides oxygen for the earth, corals do the same for the oceans. Typically, deep oceans do not have a lot of plants or trees for that matter, producing oxygen, so coral reefs produce much needed oxygen for the oceans to keep many of its species alive. The surface layer of the ocean is teething with photosynthetic plankton, though invisible to the naked eye, they produce more oxygen than the largest Redwoods, or that of our rain forests. Coral polyps, the animals primarily responsible for building reefs, can take many forms, such as large reef building colonies of different shapes, colors and sizes, graceful flowing fans, and even small solitary organisms. They all work together to create this amazing infrastructure and complex ecosystem. Coral reefs mainly form in the tropics, since they favor temperatures between 70 – 80 degrees Fahrenheit, and they also tend to develop well in the areas with a lot of sunlight, because the individual polyps which contribute to the growth of the reef, contains symbiotic algae.

Unfortunately, global warming has caused, and continues to cause, the destruction of many coral reefs, because of the increase in water temperatures. This rise in temperature causes the corals to expel the symbiotic algae living in their tissues, which are responsible for maintaining their vibrant colors. A spike of 1 – 2 degrees Celsius in ocean temperatures, sustained over several weeks, can lead to bleaching. If corals are bleached for prolonged periods, they will eventually die. According to the "International Panel on Climate Change", so far, the oceans have taken up about 90 % of the excess heat generated by human caused global warming. Even if emissions are aggressively curtailed, the oceans will continue heating up for decades to come. The oceans are also acidifying, as they soak up an estimated 20-30% of human generated carbon emissions, and as carbon dioxide dissolves into these waters, their PH plummets. Let's all do whatever we possibly can to limit, reduce and eventually eradicate these conditions, that are constantly adding to an already increasing global warming and destruction of our planet's coral reefs.

Reference Scripture: Genesis 1:20-22- (NLT)

Prayer

Lord God, You are indeed a Creative genius. You created the earth and everything in it, even the oceans and the millions of marine lives within it. When I see underwater structures such as coral reefs, I am always in awe of its immense beauty and complexity. Please grant mankind the wisdom to put a stop to the very behaviors that are damaging our planet's climate and coral reefs. Amen.

ACKNOWLEDGEMENTS

First and foremost, I thank God Almighty, who is the absolute source of my life, strength, and salvation. God has instilled in me the desire, inspiration, and vision, to put my love of writing and poetry, towards the creation of "Poetic Reverence". My deepest gratitude to my mother, Merna Raymond, who has always supported and encouraged my dreams and aspirations throughout my life. She has played a pivotal role in acquiring the necessary resources and funding that helped towards the completion of this book, as well as my sister, Kitanya Raymond, for being such a loving and supportive sister in so many ways. I would also like to thank my Wife, Yvette Frith-Raymond for being that solid rock and anchor in my life, and children, Malachi, and Elasia Raymond, for their continued support and patience throughout the entire research and writing process.

Thanks to my dear friend, Mychal Umi Cox, who is a fellow poet and an accomplished Author, for the years of friendship, transparency, and sound advice. Accolades to one of my dearest friends, Diane Cedeno and Nikesha Clarke, for their years of friendship, encouragement, and financial resources. To my cousin Charles Utti, for his continued kind words of encouragement and networking resources that has helped to guide this venture. Also, to my Pastor, Dennis Dillon, who is the founder and Editor in Chief of "The Christian Times", and who is also an accomplished author, for his professional input, direction, and much appreciated prayers. To all my relatives and extended network of friends, who have supported me in fulfilling my dream, and for their varied human and financial resources. Again, my deepest gratitude to you all.

ABOUT THE AUTHOR

Doyle (Bobby) Raymond is a husband and father of two super energetic and extremely creative children. He is a "bonafide" food connoisseur and professional chef, who has worked in the New York restaurant scene for many years, including Le Parker Meridien and other prominent establishments. His deep love and passion for creative writing and poetry began at a very young age, where he would read his favorite books, then recite in spoken word to his family and friends. He would also enjoy creative writing and would often write poems about things he saw in and around his neighborhood. His desire to entertain others with his extensive palette of signature dishes, extends to the great outdoors, where catering events and Barbecues are part of his norm. He also enjoys sporting activities with his children, such as biking, skating, and throwing Frisbee in the local park. Being a firm believer in God and The Lord Jesus Christ, has influenced the development of "Poetic Reference", to inspire, encourage and uplift its readers, and hopefully draw them a bit closer to God, our Creator.

Printed in the United States
by Baker & Taylor Publisher Services